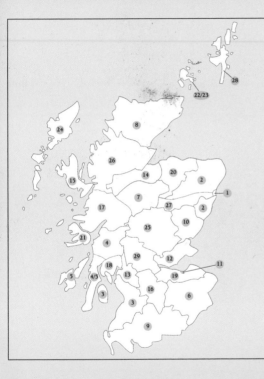

1. Aberdeen
2. Aberdeenshire
3. Arran & Ayrshire
4. Argyll
5. Southern Argyll
6. The Borders
7. The Cairngorms
8. Caithness & Sutherland
9. Dumfries and Galloway
10. Dundee & Angus
11. Edinburgh
12. Fife, Kinross & Clackmannan
13. Glasgow
14. Inverness
15. The Isle of Skye
16. Lanarkshire
17. Lochaber
18. Loch Lomond, Cowal & Bute
19. The Lothians
20. Moray
21. Mull & Iona
22. Orkney
23. Orkney in Wartime
24. The Outer Hebrides
25. Perthshire
26. Ross & Cromarty
27. Royal Deeside
28. Shetland
29. Stirling & The Trossachs

The remaining four books, Caledonia, Distinguished Deeside,
Scotland's Mountains and Scotland's Wildlife feature locations
throughout the country as suggested by the relevant captions.

PICTURING SCOTLAND

THE OUTER HEBRIDES

NESS PUBLISHING

2 Dawn breaks over Loch Seaforth, Harris. From this viewpoint (looking north into Lewis) it appears landlocked, but Loch Seaforth is in fact the greatest of several sea lochs that extend their watery

THE OUTER HEBRIDES

tentacles deep into the hinterlands of the islands that make up the Outer Hebrides.

Welcome to the Outer Hebrides!

Among the many worlds of Scotland, the Outer Hebrides (or Western Isles) must be one of the most other-worldly realms of this diverse nation. Lying off the north-west coast of Scotland, this archipelago of over 200 islands stretches around 130 miles from north to south.

The 15 inhabited islands support a resident population of about 26,500, making this region one of the least densely populated parts of Scotland. Despite great differences between the various islands, what they have in common is water – lots of it! This watery world contains over 6,000 lochs. Small wonder then that the Outer Hebrides are also abundant in a great variety of wildlife: seabirds, freshwater birds, seals, otters and whales can all be seen on and around the islands. Low-lying western coastal areas are the location of the machair, the grassy dune-land formed by wind-blown shell sand from around 3000BC onwards, which comes alive in spring with a carpet of flowers.

This is indeed another world, separated by more than sea from mainland Scotland. Here, the voices of the distant past still speak loud and clear through the numerous remnants of ancient societies. Traces of the Neolithic, Bronze and Iron Ages rub shoulders in vying for our attention.

The machair: a close look at some of the flowers that make up this colourful carpet in spring and early summer. Inset: a clover flower in detail.

Stone circles, standing stones, brochs and burial cairns can be found in abundance throughout the islands. The main focus of Neolithic activity is the astonishing network of stone circles in and around Calanais. The principal site presents an awesome array of intricately arranged stones that grips the attention of visitors from all over the world.

Early Christian sites also abound, dating from the 6th century onwards. Evidence of the Norse empire is plentiful in place names and archaeological remains. The Gaels, present long before the Norse invaders, managed to survive the tenure of these overlords (which ended in 1266) and today their culture remains a major influence. The Gaelic language is still widely spoken and the islands' indigenous music has developed an international following.

The Outer Hebrides are now officially known by their Gaelic name, Na h-Eileanan Siar. Indeed, the Gaelic names for all the islands take precedence on official signage, so it is useful to know what they are when travelling. Therefore, they are included in brackets in the following paragraph which sets out the plan of this book. Although they look very different in Gaelic, their pronunciation is similar to the English.

6   This carving is thought to be of St Clement in Rodel church (see pages 58/59).

Our photographic tour begins in Stornoway (Steòrnabhagh), the capital of the islands, located on the east coast of the island of Lewis (Leodhais). From here it explores the northern reaches of Lewis before heading south-west to the antiquity-laden area around Callanish (Calanais). A trip to the island of Great Bernera follows, then south to Harris (Na Hearadh), the mountainous heart of the northern half of the Outer Hebrides. Although Lewis and Harris are thought of as separate islands, they are in fact one landmass divided by a land border. Beyond Harris a ferry crossing takes us to the southern group of islands. From north to south these are Berneray (Bhearnaraigh), North Uist (Uibhist a Tuath), Benbecula (Beinn na Faoghla), South Uist (Uibhist a Deas), and Eriskay (Eiriosgaigh). These islands are all linked by a series of causeways, but from Eriskay the final stage of our tour entails another ferry to reach Barra (Eilean Bharraigh) and Vatersay (Bhatarsaigh).

This remote western edge of Scotland exudes a world-between-worlds atmosphere, a place where a maritime environment embraces a land of ancient mystery, a land in which resident and visitor alike will succumb to its matchless, moody magnificence.

Stornoway War Memorial floodlit.　7

8 Stornoway viewed from Gallows Hill. Lews Castle, built in 1848 for Sir Charles Matheson and later the home of Lord Leverhulme, can be seen on the left. Stornoway grew up around the best natural

...arbour in the Outer Hebrides. Regular ferries serve Stornoway from Ullapool on the mainland. ...he town is a good base from which to explore Lewis. It also hosts an annual Celtic Festival.

10 The waterfront at Stornoway. The building near the centre with clocktower is the Old Town Hall. Towards the right with the blue and black turret is An Lanntair, the arts centre.

Left: the beautifully crafted Herring Girl statue by the harbour. 11
Right: a wood carving of a fisherman, also at the harbour.

12 Stornoway's harbour hosts many pleasure craft and fishing boats and a Lifeboat is also stationed there.

Seals are a fairly common sight on the more remote Outer Hebridean coasts, but this one was spotted in Stornoway harbour, keeping an eye on the photographer!

14 The Eye Peninsula stretches east from Stornoway, seen here from across Broad Bay. Tiumpan Head lighthouse is just visible on the left. Hebridean weather often provides dramatic skyscapes like this.

In 1919, returning servicemen confronted the then owner of Lewis, Lord Leverhulme, over the issue **15** of land tenure rights. This memorial at Gress (north-west of Stornoway) commemorates these events.

16 From Gress the road goes to the village of Tolsta, where the beach is noted for its array
of impressive rock stacks.

The road continues a mile or so beyond Tolsta, after which a track leads to this waterfall. **17**
Wet weather had dramatically increased the flow over the falls when this picture was taken.

18 In the north of Lewis, Clach an Truiseil (left), is the tallest standing stone in Scotland at just over 6m/20ft high. Right: remains of the Neolithic chambered cairn outside the village of Steinacleit.

Moving now to the northern-most tip of Lewis, this is the attractive haven of the Port of Ness. **19**
This is an area in which Gaelic is the language of choice for many people.

20 Nearby is the Butt of Lewis, the most northerly point of the island, noted in the Guinness Book of Records as the windiest spot in the UK. Even on relatively calm days like this, the sea crashes with

force on the rocks around the lighthouse. This famous structure, established in 1862, stands 37 metres high and its light can be seen from a distance of 25 nautical miles.

22 Left: the straight and narrow way that leads to St Moluag's Church at Eoropie, close to the Butt of Lewis. Right: a stained-glass window in the church. St Moluag was a contemporary of St Columba.

Eoropie beach – simply fabulous! There are several more beach scenes in this book, but that is because they are such a feature throughout the Outer Hebrides, and they all just beg to be photographed!

24 This is the main grouping of stones at Calanais (Calanais 1), work on which began around 2900BC. It consists of around 50 stones, comprising a circle with central monolith (middle of picture) and straight

lines of stones that run approximately north, south, east and west from the circle. The remains of a burial chamber can be seen inside the circle, with four small stones remaining upright (see also pages 32-35). **25**

26 Top: this 'blackhouse' at Arnol on the north-west coast of Lewis was occupied until 1964, yet its architecture and layout follow a tradition that goes back to the Viking period. Below: preserved remains.

Left: inside the Arnol blackhouse, complete with peat fire and spinning wheel. Right: interior of the restored Norse water-powered grain mill at Shawbost, showing the grain hopper and grindstone. **27**

28 Shawbost lies a few miles west of Arnol. The building on the right houses the mill equipment shown on the previous page, while the nearer building to the left contains a drying kiln.

Continuing south-west brings us to Garenin (Gearrannan) where blackhouse restoration has been taken a stage further, with a small village of such houses. Here, a stack of peat is drying in readiness for winter. **29**

30 Left: brochs are among Scotland's most impressive Iron Age buildings. Dun Carloway is a particularly well-preserved example. Right: staircase built between the outer and inner walls.

Before a closer look at the Calanais stone settings, a sunrise moment with the sun reflected in the loch close to the main site, Calanais 1.

32 A visit to Calanais can be rewarding at any time of year, as the seasons all bring their own light and moods to the stones. It is especially spectacular when backlit by the Aurora Borealis.

The area surrounding the main site contains a network of smaller stone circles. With Calanais 1 **33** visible in the distance, this is one of the stones at Calanais 2, known as Cnoc Ceann a' Gharraidh.

34 Near Calanais 2, this is Cnoc Fillibhir Bheag (Calanais 3), one of 11 groups around Calanais 1. This density of ritual sites suggests that they are an interdependent network.

About 1¼ miles to the south lies Calanais 4, the five-stone group known as Ceann Hulavig. **35**
From here too, Calanais 1 is visible, between the stones pictured here – see inset picture.

36 After Calanais, a visit to the isle of Great Bernera is an essential detour. Keeping right on to the end of the road at Bosta reveals this restored Iron Age house at the head of a secluded bay.

The weather is prone to sudden change – so be prepared to embrace whatever it throws at you! For **37** example, a family enjoys sunshine on the beach, while beyond the sea is rough as the storm approaches.

38 The remote west coast of Lewis is an area of scenic majesty, perhaps best exemplified by the vast extent of Uig beach (Traigh Uige) with almost two miles of golden sand.

It is a place of many moods. Here, a brisk wind has created froth that has accumulated at the limit 39
of the tide's reach and has taken on the colour of the sand.

40　Leaving Lewis behind, now it's time to explore Harris, the most rugged and mountainous part of the Outer Hebrides, as this image infers. The rising sun seen in the picture on pages 2-3 is beginning to

illuminate Glen Scaladale which leads into the mountains. The high point on the left is part of the   41
Clisham group, while the summits in the centre are Uisgneabhal Mor and Teileasbhal.

42 From the summit of Clisham (799m/2620ft), the highest hill in the Outer Hebrides, this south-westerly view includes part of the isle of Taransay on the right and the hills by Northton in the centre . . .

. . . while to the east, framed by some of the summit rocks, the panorama takes in the great fjord of **43** Loch Seaforth with the region known as Park beyond.

44 Clisham's summit ridge has many outcrops of strangely eroded rocks. The main bedrock of the Outer Hebrides is ancient Lewisian gneiss, formed up to 3,000 million years ago.

The north-westerly view from the ridge takes in the extent of the Harris hills that continue **45** for about 10 miles before descending to the sea.

46 Another day of exploring the Harris hills begins with a walk northwards up Glen Mhiabhaig towards the steep profile of Sron Scourst, prominent in the centre of the picture.

First summit of the day is Stuabhal (579m/1899ft), from where the impressive length of Loch **47** Langabhat stretches northwards for at least six miles. A passing shower obscures the horizon.

48 Facing the other way from the same spot reveals the next two peaks, Teileasbhal (697m/2286ft), left, and Uisgneabhal Mor, at 729m/2391ft the second-highest hill in the Outer Hebrides.

The road at the southern edge of the mountains picks its way along the coast to the tiny settlement **49** of Huisinis where it ends. The uninhabited island of Scarp can be seen at top right.

50 Returning from Huisinis we come to Amhuinnsuidhe Castle. Designed in the Scottish Baronial style by the Victorian architect David Bryce, the Castle was built in 1867 for the 7th Earl of Dunmore.

The stream that flows off the hills next to Amhuinnsuidhe drops straight into the sea from **51** this waterfall, adding extra scenic charm to the bay in front of the castle.

52 The port village of Tarbert, Harris. Tarbert is a Norse word meaning a place where boats can be dragged overland between two areas of water. The main ferry route is to Uig, Isle of Skye.

Established in 2015 and located in Tarbert, the Isle of Harris Distillery is the first on the island of Harris and produces both whisky and gin. It welcomes visitors for distillery tours.

54 The Isle of Scalpay lies off the east coast of Harris, accessed via Tarbert and connected to the mainland by a bridge. This is its main settlement, clustered around South Harbour.

The district of South Harris begins at Tarbert. On the west side of South Harris lies Luskentyre
where this peaceful, wonderful beach offers rest to the weary and recreation for the young.

56 The mini-deltas, known as saltings, where rivers and burns meet the sea, are an important habitat for wading birds and wild flowers. The village of Northton is seen in the distance.

Leverburgh sits on a sheltered loch on the south coast of Harris. From here we say farewell to the
northern half of the Outer Hebrides and take the ferry to Berneray, but first a little detour to Rodel.

58 At the southern tip of South Harris is the village of Rodel, noted for St Clement's Church. Dating from the 1520s, it is built on a site where Christian worship has been practiced for up to 1,500 years.

While the outside is impressive, the carvings housed inside are rated as the finest collection of late **59** medieval sculpture surviving in the Western Isles. This is the tomb of Alexander Macleod.

60 The Outer Hebrides have been long known as a stormy environment, but these days the frequency of severe weather seems to be on the increase. This scene is at Rodel harbour.

The impressive sight of Orcas (also known as Killer Whales) can sometimes be seen **61** in Hebridean waters. Seals are among their favoured prey.

62 And so to Berneray, where the ferry from Leverburgh docks. A big Hebridean sky contrasts with the sea, glorious green due to the effect of the sand beneath.

On Berneray, a contrast between restored and unrestored ('would suit DIY enthusiast'!) cottages at **63** the hamlet of Baile – the name is Gaelic for 'township'. A causeway connects Berneray to North Uist.

64 As we begin an exploration of North Uist, the first point of interest is the well-preserved Iron Age broch of Dun an Sticir. The picture above shows how two causeways had to be crossed to reach

the broch, seen on the islet on the right, making it a very defensible site. Above is the view across the causeway from the islet on the left of the picture opposite that leads to the broch.

66 Another superb Traigh Mor (Gaelic for big beach), Clachan Sands in the north-facing bay near Trumisgarry, from which the Harris Hills are visible in the distance.

Taking the road that skirts the western side of North Uist brings many delights and also the sight of **67** the somewhat curious folly of Scolpaig Tower, built around 1830 on the site of an earlier dun.

68 Lochmaddy is the main village in North Uist, seen nestling under the slopes of North Lee. Among Lochmaddy's attractions is Taigh Chearsabhagh, an award-winning Museum and Arts Centre.

Much is said about the light in the Outer Hebrides. This sunrise in Lochmaddy gives a good idea why! **69**

70 Although the Outer Hebrides tend to be a windy environment, evening can often bring calmer moments that allow scenes like this. The road from Lochmaddy to Clachan offers many such images.

Further along this road is the huge Barpa Langais chambered cairn, the best preserved in the Outer 71
Hebrides and the only one to retain its original roofed chamber and passage intact. Inset: the entrance.

72 Autumn colour warms this grand vista. Taken from Blashaval, it sums up the physical geography of the Uists: water, water everywhere! Here and there outcrops of rocky hills add relief to the scene.

The pair of hills on the right is North and South Lee, neither of them very high but imposing none the less, given the flatlands that flank them. South Lee is the higher at 281m/921ft.

74 Not far from Barpa Langais cairn is the largest stone circle in the Uists. Its name, Pobull Fhinn, means Fingal's People, a reference to a hero of early Gaelic literature (approach via Langais Lodge Hotel).

Frequent rain showers make for frequent rainbows. This double one was captured over Loch Euphort while en route to a very wet walk to climb Eabhal, North Uist's highest hill at 347m/1138ft.

76 Eabhal stands in the isolated south-east corner of North Uist and reaching it entails the crossing of what is often very wet ground. It is also necessary to cross the outflow of Loch Obasaraigh,

but the rewards are spectacular! This is the view to the north across Loch Obasaraigh and Loch Euphort, with the hills of Burrabhal, middle distance on the right, and the Lees beyond.

78 The Uists are rich in ecclesiastical remains. The Church of the Holy Trinity at Carinish has recently undergone a degree of renovation. It was an important place of learning in the early medieval period.

The next main island is Benbecula. This view from Eabhal looking west shows the shallow sea inlet 79
that separates it from North Uist – at low tide more sandbank and channel than open sea.

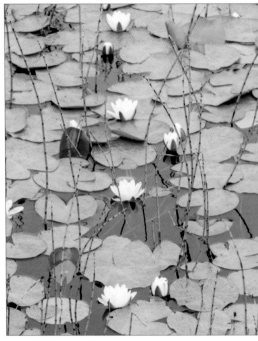

80 Left: Benbecula lies between North Uist and South Uist and is equally watery – good for dramatically reflected sunsets. Right: water-lilies in a Benbecula lochan. They are abundant in the Outer Hebrides.

Borve Castle, Benbecula, built by the MacRuairis. Its date of construction is not known, but by the **81** middle of the 14th century it was the most important castle in the Outer Hebrides.

82 A little north of Borve, Nunton's beach plays host to a number of oystercatchers. Despite the name, their diet is not limited to oysters.

Left: further along the beach, sanderlings forage for food. Right: gannets make a spectacular sight **83** as they dive for fish.

84 Left: after crossing the causeway from Benbecula to South Uist the first point of interest is the 9m/30ft tall Our Lady of the Isles statue, erected in 1957. Right: a restored cottage at Howmore.

Loch Druidibeag, one of the larger freshwater lochs on South Uist, is a nature reserve. Beyond, the **85** mountains of Hecla, Beinn Choradail and Beinn Mhor look both appealing and intimidating.

86 Up amongst those peaks, from Beinn Mhor we look across to Beinn Choradail (527m/1729ft) on the right and Hecla (or Thacla, 606m/1988ft) in the distance.

At 620m/2034ft, Beinn Mhor is the highest point on South Uist and boasts a long and precipitous **87** ridge. For the height of the hill it is quite a tough trek due to the long and boggy walk-in.

88 The complex of church and chapel remains at Howmore take on a warm glow in the low evening sun. It is not known when building began, but the style of an incised stone cross found here

suggests it could have been a place of worship by, or even before, the 9th century. The structure near the centre of the picture is the remnant of Caibeal Dhiarmaid – St Dermot's Chapel.

90 Just to the north and within sight of the Howmore ruins, Castle Bheagram stands on its island in Loch an Eilein. It is a medieval structure that might have been used as a vantage point or refuge.

Moving a few miles south to Bornais, on a point jutting into the sea is Dun Vulan, an Iron Age **91** broch. Excavations revealed that what we see now is the remnant of a tower once 4.5m/15ft tall.

92 Left: memorial to Flora MacDonald, born in this area, who went on to aid Bonnie Prince Charlie after Culloden. Right: Beinn a'Charra standing stone is positioned on the slopes that lead to Beinn Mhor.

A pair of roundhouse footings at the Bronze Age settlement of Cladh Hallan near Dalabrog. Occupation **93** of the site goes back to 2200BC, although these structures are more recent, from around 1000BC.

94 The roundhouses on the previous page were part of a larger settlement close to the sea. Generation upon generation of people will have walked on this beach and enjoyed these wonderful sunsets.

From Dalabrog the main road turns east to reach the village and ferry port of Lochboisdale, seen **95** here from Ben Kenneth. The village was established from about 1838 as a result of land clearances.

96 From Dalabrog one can also continue south to Pollacher. The anglicised version of the village's name comes from the Gaelic, Pol a Charra, which refers to the standing stone here.

Left: the Sound of Eriskay is where the *SS Politician* sank with its cargo of whisky in 1941, **97**
the event that inspired the film *Whisky Galore*. Right: the causeway from South Uist to Eriskay.

98 The village of Am Baile on Eriskay. The Isle of Eriskay is where Bonnie Prince Charlie first set foot on Scottish soil, in July 1745, having sailed from France.

St Michael's Church in Am Baile has various links with the sea, including this boat prow built into **99** the altar table (see lower centre of picture). It comes from a lifeboat that belonged to HMS *Hermes*.

100 A 45-minute crossing from Eriskay brings us to Barra. In the north of the island, lie the remains of Cille Bharra, the church of Saint Barr. The surrounding churchyard remains in use.

Barra Airport is the only one in Britain where the runway is the beach! Flight schedules have to take **101** account of the tides. Here, a flight to Glasgow has just lifted off.

102 Its beaches are one of Barra's claims to fame, justifiably so, and this one at Borve on the west of the island is perhaps the best. (With thanks to the ladies in the picture who allowed it to be used.)

Castlebay is the village capital of Barra. It is set around a sheltered bay on the south of the island. **103**
On the right, Kisimul Castle perches on an islet in the bay.

104 Taking time out from our stay on Barra to flit over the causeway to neighbouring Vatersay,
   we indulge in one more beach scene, as the curved strand here provides such a tremendous view.

But of course it's not always like this – there are storms too. Back in 1853 a very severe one caused the emigrant ship *Annie Jane* to strike Vatersay rocks and sink with the loss of 333 lives.

106 Beyond Vatersay a string of small islands continues southwards. The most spectacular of these is Mingulay, with its huge cliffs and sea caves. It can be visited by boat from Barra.

ack on Barra, superb views of the whole of the island can be enjoyed from Heaval, the 383m/1256ft **107** hill above Castlebay. The Virgin and Child statue looks down over the village.

108 Looking down from Heaval to the east shows a more rugged but still attractive side to the island, where a string of small settlements cluster round the sheltered bays.

The oldest parts of Kisimul Castle may go back to the early 1400s, but it has been greatly restored **109** and rebuilt, a task completed in 1970. Inset: Barra's modern War Memorial.

110 Castlebay at night. The ferry *Lord of the Isles* has just docked after its voyage of almost five hours from Oban.

The same ferry about to depart the following morning. There are some glum faces on board, 111 but then, they are about to leave Barra . . .

Published 2016 by Ness Publishing, 47 Academy Street, Elgin, Moray, IV30 1LR
Phone 01343 549663 www.nesspublishing.co.uk
(First edition published 2011, reprinted 2012, 2013 & 2014, second edition 2015)

All photographs © Colin & Eithne Nutt except p.5 (main) © www.virtualheb.co.uk;
p.32 © Emma Mitchell; p.52 © www.undiscoveredscotland.co.uk; p.53 © Lawrence Winram;
p.61 © Andy Foote; p.83 (right) © Wild Ocean Photography; p.106 © Colin Palmer

Text © Colin Nutt
ISBN 978-1-906549-64-0

Front cover: Calanais standing stones; p.1: enjoying Huisinis beach; p.4: potential Harris Tweed;
this page: still enjoying Huisinis beach!; back cover: Borve beach, Barra

For a list of websites and phone numbers please turn over >

Websites and phone numbers (where available) for featured places in alphabetical order:

Amhuinnsuidhe Castle: www.amhuinnsuidhe.com (T) 01859 560200
An Lanntair Arts Centre: www.lanntair.com (T) 01851 708480
Arnol Blackhouse: www.historic-scotland.gov.uk (T) 01851 710395
Barra Airport: www.hial.co.uk/barra-airport (T) 01871 890212
Barra: www.isleofbarra.com
Benbecula: www.isle-of-benbecula.co.uk
Borve Castle: canmore.org.uk/site/9962/benbecula-borve-castle
Butt of Lewis: www.nlb.org.uk/LighthouseLibrary/Lighthouse/Butt-of-Lewis
Calanais standing stones: www.callanishvisitorcentre.co.uk (T) 01851 621422
Caledonian Macbrayne: www.calmac.co.uk (T) 0800 066 5000
Cladh Hallan: www.shef.ac.uk/archaeology/research/cladh-hallan
Dun Carloway Broch: www.historic-scotland.gov.uk (T) 01851 710395
Dun Vulan: canmore.org.uk/site/9825
Eriskay: www.visitouterhebrides.co.uk/our-islands/isles-of-south-uist-and-eriskay/eriskay
Garenin Blackhouse Village: www.gearrannan.com (T) 01851 643416
Harris Distillery: www.harrisdistillery.com (T) 01859 502212
Harris Tweed: www.harristweedhebrides.com (T) 01851 702862
Harris: www.explore-harris.com
Howmore church ruins: www.visitouterhebrides.co.uk/see-and-do/howmore-tobha-mhor-ancient-chapels
Lewis: www.isle-of-lewis.com
North Uist: www.isle-of-north-uist.co.uk
Shawbost Norse Mill: www.visitouterhebrides.co.uk/see-and-do/norse-mill-and-kiln
South Uist: www.southuist.com
St Clement's Church: www.explore-harris.com/attractions/historical-attractions/church-of-st-clement
St Moluag's Church: www.canmore.org.uk/site/4419/lewis-eoropie-teampull-mholuaidh-st-moluags-church
Stornoway: www.stornoway-lewis.co.uk
The Outer Hebrides: www.visitouterhebrides.co.uk